G000079051

COOKIE
CLUB

THE COOKIE CLUB COOKBOOK

14 RECIPES FOR FABULOUS CAKES AND BAKES

Our Charities

Exeter Foundation
The Exeter Foundation was established in 2011 by the Exeter Rugby Club Executive and local business as a fundraising body committed to supporting the Greater Exeter region. It is a vehicle that helps many local charities, channeling funding from rugby related activities in a structured way. Since founding, the charity has raised over £1m and helped over 80 projects and charities.

Devon Air Ambulance
Devon Air Ambulance provides an essential and life saving service to the region in delivering its mission to "to relieve sickness and injury in and around the county of Devon through provision of an emergency Air Ambulance Service." The charity needs to raise £5.5million per annum to cover operating costs, with funding on top of that needed for capital spend.

Contents

Introduction

As a professional rugby player who has spent ten amazing years with Exeter, I am proud to have been awarded a Testimonial Year for 2018/19. Two characteristics, pride and passion, epitomise all that is exceptional about our Rugby Club and the supporters. Without doubt they have fuelled our era of success and I have been extremely lucky to have played a small part in the amazing rise of the team. This is a once in a lifetime opportunity for me to give something back for the support and encouragement I have received from all those around me.

I have nominated two local charities to benefit from my year and this book; Devon Air Ambulance and the Exeter Foundation. The work of both charities make a significant difference to everyone in the area – I am immensely proud to support them both.

So many people have already contributed to making this year a success. I will forever be indebted to my Testimonial Year committee for the tremendous amount of work they have put in to all of the projects and events, including this book. They are Mike Blakeley, Paul West, Tracey Duke, Peter and Cathy Barlett-Horwood, Verdum Trott, Lisa Singleton, Marc Ashley and Debbie and Holly from Mad Cakes.

In making the book I am grateful to my fellow Cookie Club members and the other players that have been involved. My thanks also go to Debbie from Mad Cakes in Exeter and her team for all of the efforts to check, rewrite and bake the recipes. I'd also like to thank Jack Nowell for sneaking in the rival Sandwich Club recipe to provide some savoury balance. To Phil Mingo for the photography, Ali Myer for the design and layout, James Woollam for overseeing the publishing and Ingram Content Group for their support in printing and distribution. Finally, to Paul West and RGB/The Room Works for their ongoing support and sponsorship of this book. We couldn't have done it without you.

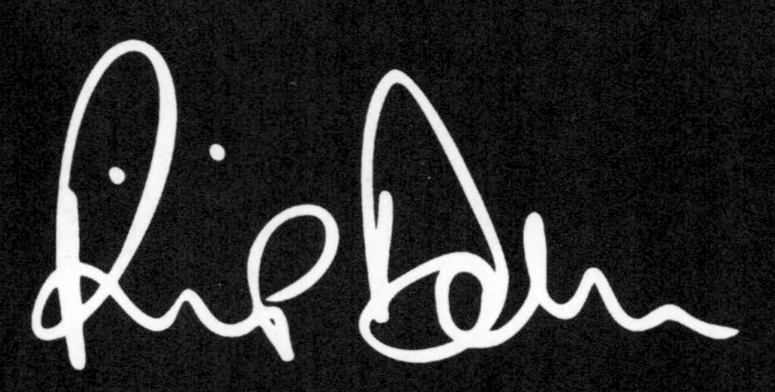

the
room
works
NISBETS

Christine's Chocolate Rugby Balls

Christine was the winner of our auction to have her recipe appear in the this book.

Ingredients

- 175g organic wholemeal flour
- 75g organic muesli
- ½ tsp bicarbonate of soda
- 30g organic dried apricots, soaked overnight then chopped into small pieces
- 175g organic butter
- 175g organic dark brown soft sugar
- 200g organic plain cooking chocolate
- 1 tube of white chocolate icing or royal icing

Method

- Preheat the oven to 160°C (140°C fan oven, gas mark 3, 325°F).

1. Mix the flour, muesli, bicarbonate of soda and chopped apricots in a bowl.
2. Rub in the butter with fingers as if making pastry, then stir in the sugar.
3. Spoon the mixture into an even layer in two round sponge tins or a greased 28cm x 18cm Swiss roll tin.
4. Bake for 30 minutes, remove from the oven and leave to cool in the tin.
5. Melt the chocolate and pour over the cake. Leave to set.
6. Cut into rugby ball shapes or squares.
7. Decorate the rugby balls with white chocolate icing or royal icing.

Thomas Waldrom's Rocky Road

'Thomas the Tank' has moved on from Exeter but was a founding member of the Cookie Club. The book simply wouldn't have been complete without him. So much so he managed to get not one but two recipes into this book. The mark of a true professional cookie club member. This recipe is an all round winner.

Ingredients

- 300g milk chocolate
- 200g dark chocolate
- 100g white chocolate chips
- 60g mini marshmallows
- 100g crushed digestive biscuits
- 250g mixed chocolates and sweets

Method

- Preheat the oven to 180°C (160°C fan oven, gas mark 4, 350°F).

1. Melt the milk and dark chocolate slowly.
2. In a separate bowl, mix all of the other ingredients.
3. Line a 20cm square tin with parchment paper. Spread the sweet ingredients into the lined tin and pour the melted chocolate over the top, ensuring it is spread evenly.
4. Refrigerate for a couple of hours or overnight.

Chef's Tip

FOR A SLIGHTLY HEALTHIER ALTERNATIVE, USE DRIED FRUIT AND CHOPPED NUTS INSTEAD OF SWEETS AND BISCUITS.

Dave's Carrot Cake Cheesecake Cake

This moist and delicious take on the traditional carrot cake will take a little preparation. You might get into a ruck making it, but boy is it worth it.

Ingredients

For the carrot cake layers:

- 400g caster sugar
- 250ml oil (light olive oil works best here)
- 4 large eggs
- 250g plain flour
- 1 tsp bicarbonate of soda
- 1 tsp baking powder
- ¼ tsp salt
- 2 tsp ground cinnamon
- 170g grated carrots

For the cheesecake layer:

- 200g cream cheese, softened
- 200g caster sugar
- ¼ tsp salt
- 2 large eggs
- 250ml soured cream
- 75ml whipping cream

For the frosting:

- 225g unsalted butter, softened
- 100g cream cheese, softened
- 1 tsp vanilla extract
- 60ml double cream
- 500g icing sugar
- 100g chopped pecans

Method

- Preheat the oven to 180°C (160°C fan oven, gas mark 4, 350°F).
- Prepare a 9 inch springform pan by wrapping the bottom (outside) with a double layer of foil. Line the bottom of the pan (inside) with a circle of parchment paper.
- Grease and flour two 9 inch cake pans.

For the cheesecake layer:

1. Add 1 inch of water to a large roasting pan and place it in the lower part of the oven to preheat.
2. Beat the cream cheese with the caster sugar for 2-3 minutes until creamy. Add the salt and beat well, then add the eggs and beat well again.
3. Beat in the soured cream and whipping cream until light and fluffy (about 2 minutes). Pour into the 9 inch springform pan.
4. Place the pan in the centre of the preheated roasting pan, being careful not to spill the water.
5. Bake for 45 minutes. Turn the oven off and let the cheesecake sit in the oven for an additional 30 minutes. Remove and cool completely on counter.
6. When cooled, remove the outside portion of the springform tin and place in the freezer for at least 2 hours or overnight, or in the refrigerator for up to 24 hours.

For the carrot cake layers:

1. In a large mixing bowl, combine the sugar, oil and eggs until blended.
2. Add in the flour, bicarbonate of soda, baking powder, salt and cinnamon. Beat for about 2 minutes. Add in the grated carrots.
3. Pour into the prepared cake tins.
4. Bake for 30 minutes.
5. Cool on a wire rack for 10 minutes. Remove from pans and cool completely.

For the frosting:

1. In a large mixing bowl, combine the cream cheese and butter, beating with a whisk attachment for 3 minutes.
2. Add in the sugar, vanilla and double cream.
3. Beat for a further 3-4 minutes until light and fluffy.
4. Fold in the chopped pecans.

Bringing it together:

- To assemble the cake, lay one layer of carrot cake, then add the cheesecake and top with the second layer of carrot cake. Spread on the frosting, first on the sides and then on top.
- The cake can be stored in the refrigerator, covered, for up to 3 days.

Chef's Tip

PREPARE THE CHEESECAKE LAYER FIRST. THIS CAN BE DONE EARLIER IN THE DAY, OR THE NIGHT BEFORE. THE CHEESECAKE CAN BE STORED FOR 1-2 WEEKS IN THE FREEZER.

Matt's Pretty Perfect Victoria Sponge

What afternoon tea wouldn't be complete without a Victoria Sponge? This recipe is a beautiful, cloud-like, taste sensation with a fruity, creamy centre.

Ingredients

- 225g butter, at room temperature, plus a little extra to grease the tins
- 225g caster sugar, plus a little extra for dusting the finished cake
- 4 free-range eggs
- 225g self-raising flour
- 2 tsp baking powder
- Good-quality strawberry or raspberry jam
- Whipped double cream (optional)

Method

- Preheat the oven to 180°C (160°C fan oven, gas mark 4, 350°F).

1. Cream together the butter and sugar until it is light and fluffy.
2. In a separate bowl, sift the flour and baking powder together.
3. Add the flour to the butter mixture, alternating with the eggs and mix well by hand or with an electric mixer.
4. Grease and line two 20 inch loose-bottomed cake tins, divide the mixture between the two tins and smooth the surface of the cakes.
5. Bake for 20-25 minutes until the cakes are light brown and springy to touch.
6. Cool in their tins for 5 minutes before turning out onto a rack to completely cool.
7. Spread one side with the jam and cream if using, sandwich together and sprinkle with a little caster sugar to decorate.

Chef's Tip

IF YOU WANT TO GET ORGANISED AND MAKE THIS AHEAD OF TIME, LET THE CAKES COMPLETELY COOL, WRAP EACH ONE IN CLINGFILM OR FREEZER BAGS AND POP IN THE FREEZER FOR UP TO 6 MONTHS.

Tom's Brownie Delight

A squidgy, scrum-my, crunchy, chocolate lover's dream.
This recipe makes 12-16 brownies.

Ingredients

For the brownie layer:
- 150g unsalted butter
- 250g caster sugar
- 95g cocoa powder
- ½ tsp salt
- 2 tsp vanilla extract
- 2 large eggs
- 65g self-raising flour

For the Oreo layer:
- 1-2 packs of Oreo cookies (regular stuffed or double stuffed)

For the cookie dough layer:
- 110g unsalted butter, at room temperature
- 110g brown sugar
- 150g white sugar
- 1 egg
- 1¼ tsp vanilla extract
- 155g plain flour
- ½ tsp salt
- ½ tsp bicarbonate of soda
- ½ tsp baking powder
- 150g semi-sweet chocolate chips

Method

- Preheat the oven to 180°C (160°C fan oven, gas mark 4, 350°F).

For the brownie layer:
1. In a medium-sized saucepan, melt the butter over medium high heat.
2. Once melted, add the sugar and cocoa powder.
3. Whisk to combine and remove from the heat.
4. Add the salt, vanilla and eggs, and continuously whisk until the eggs are combined.
5. Add the flour and continue to mix using a wooden spoon.
6. Set the batter aside.

For the cookie dough layer:
1. Cream together the butter and sugars in a mixer.
2. Add the egg and vanilla, making sure to scrape down the sides of the mixing bowl.
3. Add the flour, salt, bicarbonate of soda and baking powder. Mix on a low speed until everything is incorporated.
4. Fold in the chocolate chips.
5. Set the dough aside.

Assembly (where the magic happens):
1. Line a 9 inch x 9 inch baking tin with baking paper.
2. Spread the cookie dough on the bottom of the baking tin, pressing down to form the bottom layer of the brownies.

3. Add a layer of Oreos to fit on top of the cookie dough. No need to overlap – one single layer will suffice.
4. Pour the brownie batter on top of the Oreo layer and make sure it is evenly spread.
5. Bake for 30-40 minutes.

To serve:

- Let the brownies rest for at least 2 hours before serving.
- Sprinkle with icing sugar and serve with ice cream for an added treat.

Thomas Waldrom's Strawberry Puffs

You can't go wrong with a good old-fashioned strawberry puff and the Tank's version doesn't go too far wrong.

Ingredients

For the choux pastry:
- 125g self-raising flour
- 100ml milk
- 100ml water
- 10g sugar
- ½ tsp salt
- 80g unsalted butter
- 2 eggs

For the filling:
- 470ml double cream
- 40g icing sugar (plus extra for decoration)
- 1 tsp vanilla extract
- Fresh strawberries, cut into slices

Method

- Preheat the oven to 180°C (160°C fan oven, gas mark 4, 350°F).

For the choux pastry:
1. In a saucepan bring the milk, water, sugar, salt and butter to a boil.
2. Remove from heat, add the flour all at once and incorporate, mixing energetically with a wooden spoon until homogenous. Make sure not to overbeat or the pastry will become tough.
3. Return the saucepan to a low heat and cook for 1-2 minutes, stirring continuously, to pull out the moisture from the batter until it pulls away from the sides of the pan (you will see that some of the dough sticks to the bottom of the pan).
4. Transfer the batter to a large bowl and allow to cool slightly.
5. Add the eggs, one at a time, carefully incorporating each into the batter using a wooden spoon or a stand mixer. It will result in a smooth batter that still holds its shape.
6. Fit a piping bag with a large ½ inch round nozzle and pipe the dough into 1-1½ inch circles on a lined baking sheet.
7. Bake in the preheated oven for 25-30 minutes or until lightly browned and puffed.
8. Remove from the oven and prick each puff with a skewer to release steam before allowing to cool on a wire rack.

For the filling:
1. In a large bowl, whip the cream with an electric mixer until it forms stiff peaks.
2. Add the icing sugar and vanilla extract. Mix to combine.

Assembly:
1. Split the cream puffs in half and fill them with the vanilla cream mixture and strawberry slices.
2. Dust with icing sugar and serve.

Ollie D's Banana Cake

Let's be honest, who doesn't love a beautiful, fragrant, banana cake? Fresh from the oven served warm with a scoop or two of vanilla ice-cream, or with your regular coffee, the banana cake is always a winner. Throw in a handful of chocolate chips at the mixing stage or a pinch of cinnamon to spice things up. You must try this recipe, it's a winner!

Ingredients

- 285g plain flour
- 1 tsp bicarbonate of soda
- ½ tsp salt
- 110g butter (plus extra for greasing)
- 225g caster sugar
- 2 free range eggs
- 4 ripe bananas, mashed to a pulp
- 85ml buttermilk
- 1 tsp vanilla extract

Method

- Preheat the oven to 180°C (160°C fan oven, gas mark 4, 350°F).

1. Sift the flour, bicarbonate of soda and salt into a mixing bowl.
2. In a separate bowl cream together the butter and sugar until light and fluffy.
3. Add the eggs, mashed bananas, buttermilk and vanilla extract to the butter and sugar mixture and mix well.
4. Fold in the flour mixture.
5. Pour the mixture into an 8 inch x 5 inch greased and lined cake tin.
6. Bake for an hour until risen and golden brown.
7. Remove from the oven and cool in the tin for a few minutes before turning out onto a wire rack.

Chef's Tip

If you don't have buttermilk just add 1½ tsp of lemon juice or vinegar to 85ml milk.

Extra Tip!

Make some cinnamon butter by spreading a tablespoon of unsalted butter onto greaseproof paper and freeze until hard. Mix a teaspoon of dark brown sugar with half a teaspoon of cinnamon and spread over butter. Roll up the butter into a log shape and cut into slices. Add this to a warm slice of Ollie's Banana Cake and enjoy!

A Little Bit About Phil

Family, Friends and Home

Family and friends have always been an important part of my life and the move out of Wales back in 2009 was difficult because of those strong everyday connections. I know Exeter isn't too far but, being much younger, stepping into the unknown away from people who were a part of your life and always there to support you was tough.

Laura was wonderful. We first met in Cardiff in 2003 and were married in the beautiful and romantic surroundings of Sorrento in Italy. It did not take long for Devon to become home. We have two daughters. Lucia, born in Cardiff in 2010, and Mia, born in Exeter in 2013. As they grow and become more settled in school our circle of friends has expanded. It is difficult not to fall in love with Devon. The proudest moments for Laura and I are to share in the enjoyment of our daughters lives; sitting in the audience in a packed theatre watching ballet performances can be emotional for all the right reasons. To see the girls run out at the Twickenham final in 2017, and how they loved doing it, would make any parent have to wipe away a tear of joy. Both of them cried at the final whistle.

Cooking

Who would have ever believed I would have my name put on a cookbook! I actually do a lot of cooking for the family and it is something I really enjoy. The "judges" sitting around the family dinner table seem to appreciate the majority of food I cook, even Lucia and Mia. My recipes have to steer away from anything too spicy, as my daughters' taste buds haven't quite matured fully yet.

Cheese

Caerphilly Rugby Football Club is a relative newcomer to Welsh Rugby (well sort of). The club was initially founded at the end of the nineteenth century but the round ball took over as the primary sport in the area, so the rugby side faded. In September 1950, 26 men met at Virginia Park to resurrect the rugby club and it was re-named Caerphilly Harlequins. The name Harlequins was dropped in 1954 and Caerphilly RFC emerged – their nickname is The Cheesemen. So what is the reason for including Caerphilly RFC in this book? Well, my rugby journey started on the turf of Caerphilly as a squat five-year-old prop and that is where the roots of the player I am today started. Although it seemed, as my body developed over the years, I wasn't destined for the front row.

What If....

When you face disappointment, it can hurt a lot. Those occasions have been times I have evaluated my goals. For example, it was a huge disappointment to be let go by the Dragons. I knew that a contract wasn't going to be, so looked around and noticed Exeter were in need of a utility back. I haven't looked back since.

Missing out on the Wales summer tour 2017 was very tough to deal with. It was such a huge rollercoaster couple of weeks, winning and scoring in the Twickenham final against Wasps, but then picking up an injury that would put a halt to my boyhood dream. It was emotionally very challenging but I wouldn't change the end result if I had the chance to do it all over again. It is going through and having to deal with those emotions that makes me stronger mentally. All those setbacks have helped me to progress my rugby career.

Pride

It wasn't until I made a few appearances for the Dragons that I actually thought I was good enough to make a career in rugby. I'm proud Exeter wanted me and that Rob Baxter once said I was his best signing. I'm very proud to have played a hand in winning silverware. I'm proud of beating Bristol to gain promotion. I'm proud of winning the Premiership final at Twickenham and I'm proud of being called up by Wales for that summer tour.

From a pure rugby perspective, the proudest moment of my time over the last 10 years was being nominated for Player's Player of the Year. The shortlist was Dave Ewers, Ben Moon and me. I didn't win that day but it certainly meant a lot to me; more even than winning medals or games. To get that recognition from your peers is simply stunning.

COOKIE CLUB

Dolly's G 'n' T Cake

A true testimonial to any gin and cake lover. This moist cake makes a great afternoon treat. Plus the left over gin can always be put to good use!

Ingredients

For the cake:

- 250g butter
- 325g golden caster sugar
- 4 eggs
- 250g self-raising flour
- 2 large limes, juice only
- 75ml natural yoghurt
- 75ml gin for the cake (and 75ml for the chef)
- 150ml tonic water (you can use elderflower flavour)
- 1 tsp juniper berries, lightly crushed

For the buttercream:

- 200g softened butter
- 400g icing sugar
- 2 tbsp milk
- 3 limes, zest only

To decorate:

- 2 limes, zested and cut into very thin wedges
- 1 tbsp granulated sugar
- ¼ cucumber, peeled into ribbons

Method

- Preheat the oven to 180°C (160°C fan oven, gas mark 4, 350°F).

For the cake:

1. Grease and line two 20cm cake tins.
2. Using a mixer, beat together the butter and 200g of the sugar until pale and fluffy, for around 5 minutes.
3. Add the eggs one by one, making sure they are fully incorporated before adding the next one. If the mixture looks like it might split, add a tablespoon of flour before folding in the rest of the flour.
4. Mix the natural yoghurt with the juice of one of the limes and 50ml of the gin. Add this to the cake mixture to make a thick and silky texture.
5. Split the mixture between the cake tins and bake for 35 minutes until a skewer comes out clean.
6. Make yourself a large G 'n' T with ice.
7. Make the syrup by placing the remaining sugar, tonic water, juniper berries and juice of one lime into a saucepan over medium heat. Once the sugar has dissolved, bring to the boil and cook for 5-7 minutes until it's a thick syrup.
8. Cool for 5 minutes, strain, then pour in the remaining gin and set aside.
9. Once the cake is out of the oven, allow to cool for 5 minutes, then prick all over with a skewer.
10. Liberally spoon the syrup mix over both of the cakes. Allow to cool completely in the tin.

For the buttercream:
1. Beat the butter until soft, then add the icing sugar, a little at a time to avoid a sugar cloud! Once fully incorporated, add the milk and lime zest.

Assembly:
1. To assemble, place one of the cake layers on a cake board, cover with about a third of the buttercream and sit the second cake layer on top. Cover this in just a thin coat of buttercream, then put the cake in the fridge for 30 minutes to firm up – this will make it easier to get the rest of the buttercream on smoothly.
2. Use the remaining buttercream to cover the top and sides of the cake – if you have a cake scraper use this to spread the buttercream evenly around the sides of the cake.

To decorate:
- Mix the lime zest with the sugar. Sprinkle this over the cake and finish with lime slices and cucumber ribbons.

Chef's Tip

MAKE SURE YOU HAVE A BOTTLE OF GIN, A BOTTLE OF TONIC, A LIME AND ICE CUBES TO ACCOMPANY THE BAKE. ALWAYS HELPS THE BAKE TIME PASS QUICKLY!

the
room
NISBETS

Origin of the Cream Tea

Although there is a little dispute on the actual origin, the Devon cream tea can be traced back to Tavistock's Benedictine Abbey. The Abbey was established in the 10th century. In AD 997, vikings looted and badly damaged the building. The restoration of the Abbey was undertaken by Ordulf, the Earl of Devon (it was his father, Ordgar, who had been responsible for establishing the Abbey). Ordulf was helped by local workers and, to reward them, the monks fed them bread, clotted cream and strawberry preserves. Sound familiar? Unfortunately, the Abbey did not survive King Henry VIII's 'Dissolution of the Monasteries' order in 1539. The centre of Tavistock now sits on the site with part of the remains still visible.

Afternoon Tea Anyone?

Britain probably became a nation of tea drinkers when Catherine de Braganza from Portugal married Charles II in 1662 and almost immediately started a custom of drinking tea at court. Tea was expensive and rare; the drink was seen as a luxury that only the most wealthy could afford. A second thank you goes to the Duchess of Bedford for making tea time a mid-afternoon meal and bringing the now very British custom of afternoon tea to the masses. It seems the wait between lunch and dinner (which was traditionally eaten between 8pm and 9pm) was just too long for the Duchess.

It all started when very simple tea and treats were delivered to her room to ward off her hunger. This quickly evolved into a formal dressed occasion as she invited friends to join her in her private rooms. By the middle of the 19th century, afternoon tea was an everyday occurrence for the upper classes and included tea, sandwiches, cakes, pastries, scones, cream and jam. This was also known as a Low Tea as it was served on low tables so the ladies cold relax in more comfortable chairs. A High Tea was a much heavier meal, traditionally taken between 5pm and 7pm, which the working class ate from a high table (dining tables).

Cream Tea

When the railway was opened to the Westcountry in the 1850s, it brought with it a huge influx of tourists. Visitors were keen to relax and indulge themselves in hotels, tearooms and cafés. The locals were obviously very happy to oblige and offered delicious afternoon cream teas, made with the very best local ingredients. Both those in Devon and Cornwall knew the jam had to be strawberry and the cream clotted, and that has never been in dispute. What is in dispute is which goes on first. The jam or the cream? The Devonians believe a cream tea should be made with cream on the bottom and jam on top, remaining true to its Tavistock Abbey origins. This construction of the cream tea is upside down according to those in Cornwall, who believe the only way to serve a cream tea properly is with jam first and the cream on top.

So, if all the facts are correct, did Cornwall "borrow" the Devon cream tea? In a separate argument Devon could be accused of "borrowing" the pasty. What is agreed in the great Devon v Cornwall debate over the cream tea is, no matter what goes on first, it should always be made with fresh local produce.

Ben's Devonshire Fruity Scones

Pass on this tip: it's cream before the jam.

Ingredients

- 350g self-raising flour, plus some for dusting
- ¼ tsp salt
- 1½ tsp baking powder
- 55g butter
- 30g caster sugar
- 75g sultanas or cherries
- 150ml milk
- 2 large eggs, beaten
- Jam and clotted cream to serve

Chef's Tip

ADD ANY KIND OF DRIED FRUIT FOR A CHANGE.
IF YOU CAN'T DECIDE IF IT'S JAM OR CREAM FIRST, JUST SERVE WITH A NICE SLICE OF BUTTER.

Method

- Preheat the oven to 220°C (200°C fan oven, gas mark 7, 430°F).

1. Tip the flour into a large bowl with the salt and baking powder, then mix. Add the butter, then rub in with your fingers until the mix resembles fine breadcrumbs. Stir in the sugar.
2. Put the milk into a jug and heat in the microwave for about 30 seconds until warm, but not hot. Add the vanilla and lemon juice, then set aside for a moment.
3. Put a lightly greased baking sheet in the oven.
4. Make a well in the dry mix, then add the liquid and sultanas and combine quickly with a cutlery knife – it will seem pretty wet at first. Scatter some flour onto the work surface and tip the dough out.
5. Dredge the dough and your hands with a little more flour, then fold the dough over 2-3 times until it's a little smoother. Pat into a round tin about 4cm deep.
6. Take a 5cm cutter (smooth-edged cutters tend to cut more cleanly, giving a better rise) and dip it into some flour. Plunge into the dough, then repeat until you have four scones. You may need to press what's left of the dough back into a round to cut out another four.
7. Brush the tops with a beaten egg and carefully place onto the baking tray.
8. Bake for 10 minutes until risen and golden on the top.
9. Eat warm or cold on the day of baking, generously topped with clotted cream and then jam.

Luke's Cornish Cowan-Dickie Scones

Be on the ball and spread the jam before the cream.

Ingredients

- 350g self-raising flour, plus some for dusting
- ¼ tsp salt
- 1 tsp baking powder
- 85g butter
- 3 tbsp caster sugar
- 175ml milk
- Lemon juice
- Beaten egg to glaze
- Jam and clotted cream to serve

Method

- Preheat the oven to 220°C (180°C fan oven, gas mark 6, 390°F).

1. Sieve the flour, salt and baking powder into a large bowl, then mix.
2. Add cubes of butter and rub in with your fingers until the mix resembles fine breadcrumbs. Stir in the caster sugar.
3. Put milk into a jug and heat in the microwave for about 30 seconds until warm, but not hot.
4. Add the vanilla extract and a squeeze of lemon juice, then set aside.
5. Place a baking sheet in the oven.
6. Make a well in the dry mix, then add the liquid and combine it quickly with a cutlery knife – it will seem pretty wet at first.
7. Sprinkle some flour onto the work surface and tip the dough out. Dredge the dough and your hands with a little more flour, then fold the dough over 2-3 times until it is a little smoother. Pat into a round about 4cm deep.
8. Take a 5cm cutter (smooth-edged cutters tend to cut more cleanly, giving a better rise) and dip it into some flour. Plunge into the dough, then repeat until you have four scones. You may need to press what's left of the dough back into a round to cut out another four.
9. Brush the tops with a beaten egg and carefully place onto the hot baking tray.
10. Bake for 10 minutes until risen and golden on the top.
11. Eat warm or cold on the day of baking, generously topped with jam and then clotted cream!

Chef's Tip
IF FREEZING, FREEZE ONCE COOL. DEFROST, THEN PUT IN A LOW OVEN (ABOUT 160°C/140°C FAN OVEN/ GAS MARK 3/325°F) FOR A FEW MINUTES TO REFRESH.

Don's Triangle Tart

If you like the triangular shaped chocolate, then Don's Tart is a must try. Throw in a handful of raisins if you like your treats even sweeter. This recipe makes 16 chunky triangles.

Ingredients

For the base:
- 250g butter
- 300g Rich Tea Biscuits (or digestives if you fancy them)

For the filling:
- 400g triangular chocolate bar
- 250ml double cream (300ml works too)
- 400g milk chocolate

To decorate:
- Ten 45g bars triangular chocolate bars

Method

For the base:
1. Crush the biscuits until fine.
2. Melt the butter over a low heat.
3. Add the butter to the crushed biscuits, mixing as you go.
4. Keep adding the butter until the mixture is the consistency of clay. If you can squeeze it in your hand and it doesn't break apart then it's all good.
5. Line a 20cm square tin with baking paper.
6. Press the mixture into the base and up the sides of the prepared dish. Set aside to cool.

For the filling:
1. Melt all the filling ingredients together in a bowl in the microwave.
2. Let the filling cool for a bit.

To decorate:
- Pour the filling into the prepared biscuit base. Get creative with the decoration and leave to cool or refrigerate overnight.
- Turn out and cut into 8 chunky squares. Then cut each square in half diagonally to create triangles.

Chef's Tip

You can melt the filling together in the microwave or in a bowl over simmering water. If you break the chocolate up before melting it, it melts quicker and you'll avoid burning.

COOKIE CLUB

Steeno's Malt Ball Squares

Tackle this recipe and these chunky squares will pack a punch to be sure. For a fruity twist, try throwing in a handful of raisins or dried cranberries during mixing. This recipe makes 16 chunky squares.

Method

1. Place the butter, milk chocolate and syrup in a saucepan and melt over a low heat.
2. Stir in the crushed digestives.
3. Set aside 6-10 of the Maltesers for decoration and mix the rest of them in with the digestives and chocolate mixture.
4. Spread into a 20cm square tin. Leave to cool.
5. Melt the white chocolate in a bowl over a pan of simmering water. Pour over the set mixture once it has cooled.
6. Crush the reserved Maltesers and sprinkle over the top.
7. Leave to set or put in the fridge and then cut into squares.

Ingredients

- 110g butter
- 225g milk chocolate
- 225g Maltesers or equivalent
- 225g digestive biscuits, crushed
- 3 tbsp golden syrup (or honey or maple syrup)
- 110g white chocolate

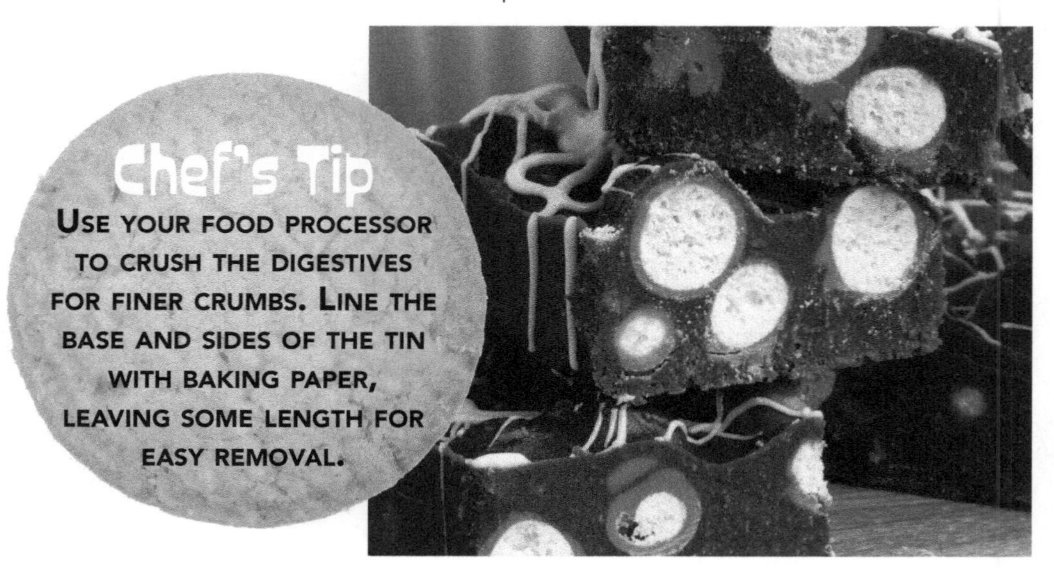

Chef's Tip

USE YOUR FOOD PROCESSOR TO CRUSH THE DIGESTIVES FOR FINER CRUMBS. LINE THE BASE AND SIDES OF THE TIN WITH BAKING PAPER, LEAVING SOME LENGTH FOR EASY REMOVAL.

Geoff Parling's Eton Mess

British and Irish Lion Geoff Parling is another former player who we couldn't miss out in this book. Here's his super, summer treat for a light finish to a meal.

Ingredients

- 2 large egg whites
- 120g caster sugar
- Pinch of cream of tartar
- 500g fresh strawberries, roughly chopped
- 450ml double cream
- 1 tbsp icing sugar

Method

- Preheat the oven to 120°C (100°C fan oven, gas mark 1, 250°F).

1. Line a large baking sheet with baking paper.
2. Whisk the egg whites in a clean bowl using an electric whisk or tabletop mixer until they reach stiff peaks.
3. Add the sugar and cream of tartar in 3 parts, re-whisking to stiff peaks each time.
4. Spoon dollops of the mixture onto the baking parchment.
5. Cook on the bottom shelf of the oven for 60-75 minutes until the meringues are completely hard and come off the paper easily.
6. Leave to cool.
7. Blitz a third of the strawberries to make a strawberry sauce.
8. In a large bowl whisk the cream with the icing sugar until it just holds its shape.
9. Roughly crush three quarters of the meringues, tip them in with the chopped strawberries and stir, then swirl through the strawberry sauce.
10. Drop into sundae glasses and crush the remaining meringues, sprinkling the pieces over the top.

Chef's Tip

For a seasonal variation, use frozen summer fruits instead of strawberries to make an unhealthy smoothie.

Moray's Gorgeous Stout Cake

Straight from the halls of chocolate cake fame, this is a gooey, squidgy, boozy piece of heaven; definitely one for the grown-ups! Don't worry if you can't eat this all at once – just keep half back and store in the fridge. This recipe makes 12 slices.

Ingredients

For the cake:
- 250ml stout
- 250g unsalted butter
- 75g cocoa powder
- 400g caster sugar
- 140ml soured cream
- 2 large eggs
- 1 tbsp vanilla extract
- 275g plain flour
- 2½ tsp bicarbonate of soda

For the topping:
- 300g cream cheese
- 150g icing sugar
- 2 tsp cornflour
- 125ml double cream

Method

- Preheat the oven to 180°C (160°C fan oven, gas mark 4, 350°F).

For the cake:
1. Pour the stout into a large saucepan, add the butter gradually and heat until the butter is melted.
2. Remove from the heat.
3. Whisk in the cocoa and sugar.
4. In a separate bowl beat the soured cream with the eggs and vanilla. Pour into the brown, buttery, beery pan.
5. Whisk in the flour and bicarbonate of soda.
6. Pour the cake batter into a greased and lined 23cm springform baking tin and bake for 45 minutes to an hour.
7. Leave the cake to cool completely in the tin on a cooling rack.
8. Once cool, place it on a plate or cake stand.

For the topping:
1. Lightly whip the cream cheese until smooth.
2. Sieve in the icing sugar and cornflour, then beat to combine.
3. If using double cream, add and beat until you have a spreadable consistency.
4. Decorate the top of the cake so that it resembles the frothy top of the famous pint.

Chef's Tip
This is quite a damp cake so leave to cool completely in the tin, on a cooling rack, before turning out.

Jack's Beefy Doorstep Sandwich

Name: Jack Nowell
Position: Winger
Your opinion of the Cookie Club: Unhealthy amateurs
Why was the sandwich club superior?: The original club. Healthy and for real athletes.
Favourite sandwich: Bacon, chicken, brie, cranberry.
Strangest thing ever eaten: Henry Slade's cooking
Last ever meal choice: Margarita pizza, basil, pesto

Method

1. Butter one side of both slices of bread, making sure to go right to the edge of the bread.
2. Add a good dollop of horseradish to one slice of the bread, butter side up.
3. Place a layer of roast beef on top.
4. Add the salad leaves and sliced tomato.
5. Add more beef and top with a dollop of mustard.
6. Take the second slice of bread and place it butter side down to top off the sandwich.
7. Cut in half, sit back and tuck in!

Ingredients

- 2 chunky slices of Jack's loaf or similar fresh white bread
- Several slices of roast beef
- Butter
- Horseradish and mustard
- Peppery salad leaves (rocket or watercress) and sliced tomato to garnish (optional)

Chef's Tip

MIX THE HORSERADIS WITH MAYONNAISE T MAKE IT A LITTLE CREAMIER.

The story behind the beef

The beef used for Jack's sandwich was reared on Exwick Barton. The farm was bought in the 1970's by the Baxter family, a name "stamped" in the walls at Exeter Rugby Club and key to the club's success. The cattle reared on the farm are pedigree Devon cattle with previous club captain and Exeter stalwart Richie Baxter very much at the helm. Richie played at Exeter for 16 seasons, amassing a huge 431 games and scoring 126 tries. The former England Under-21 international was part of the Exeter team that won promotion to the top flight of English rugby and was key to laying the foundations for the success that followed.

Richie's focus is now very much on his work around the farm, building and continuously improving the herd which are renowned for the quality of their meat from grazing in the rich Devon countryside.

Although the beef was reared on Exwick Barton, Richie has very close links with Burrow Farm located on the National Trust's stunning East Devon countryside's Killerton Estate. This 350 acre traditional mixed farm has been run by Neil and Sally Grigg since 2007. Burrow Farm is a Master Butcher and sells the Exwick Barton beef at the butchers' shop in Cowick Street, Exeter as well as at a number of local farmer's markets.

I had never heard of The Cookie Club before Paul West from The Room Works came to visit Mad Cakes a few months ago. He explained that a group of the Exeter Rugby team players gather after training each week to bake cakes and there was an idea to publish a Cookie Club recipe book for Phil's Testimonial Year. Would I help? It was never in any doubt, but little did I know what was in store!

It's not every day at Mad Cakes that we get asked to help create a cookbook. Certainly not one that documents the delights of the legendary and mysterious Cookie Club. I couldn't wait to get involved and bake lots of nutritious and healthy bakes, expecting recipes with fruit, vegetables, nuts and seeds. After all, some of these guys play for England and have to stay fit and keep trim, right? I couldn't have been more wrong, it seemed the general order of the day was to empty a sweet shop into a bowl and find something to stick it together!

Getting to work, Hollie my assistant had to be my critic as I worked my way through the recipes. Baking, tasting and tweaking them to become legendary bakes. I am a bit of a perfectionist and

I couldn't help but make a second batch of every cake to make sure they were exactly right; I knew the importance of getting the recipes right and I needed to ensure the guys best efforts could be shared time and time again by rugby and cake fans alike.

With a whirlwind 48 hours to prepare for the photo shoot, I had to not only bake each cake to precision but also think about the presentation

and props that we'd need. The shoot itself was awesome in so many ways, not least working with our brilliant photographer Phil Mingo and designer Ali Myer. I made friends for life.

Meeting and spending time with the boys at The Room Works was just fantastic. Watching them critique their own cakes and that of their peers was a great experience. If you think they are tough on the pitch, you should see their dedication to their recipes; you could really tell what a decent cake means to them.

All in all, it was the most amazing experience. Did I ever imagine I would be sharing tips and hints about cinnamon butter with Olli Devoto, or arguing the cream team debate with 2 of the nation's finest front row players? Never in a million years! I absolutely loved it and it will go down in history as one of the maddest and most crazy things that Mad Cakes have ever done.

Phil, I'm delighted I could play my part in the book and even more so that your efforts have secured you a coveted and honoured place in the Cookie Club Hall of Fame.

Wishing you a wonderful testimonial year.

Debbie x

MAD CAKES
Tel: 01392 757620 • Email: Madcakes@sky.com
Unit 12, Bakers Yard Alphin Brook Road,
Exeter, Devon EX2 8RG

The Room Works hosts sporting bake-off show down

Tel: 01392 260700
Alphinbrook Road,
Marsh Barton,
Exeter, Devon,
EX2 8RG

At The Room Works we have a history of backing Phil's baking prowess. To celebrate the first anniversary of our opening, he was joined in our showroom by fellow players Will Chudley, Haydn Thomas, Kai Horstmann and Harry Williams to do battle against a team from Exeter City FC in a charity bake-off.

Players showed off their culinary skills by using one of our displays to make cupcakes, meringues, and 15 'scrum'-ptious scones. They also had to creatively cover and decorate a cake.

We're delighted to be helping to raise further funds to support Devon Air Ambulance and Exeter Foundation with this book.

If you're looking to update your kitchen space, whether it's to create a haven for baking excellence, or the perfect family hub, pay a visit to The Room Works. Our friendly and knowledgeable team will be happy to show you our collection of high quality kitchens, and help turn your dreams into reality.

ISBN 978-1-5272-3086-6
First published in 2018 as part of the Phil Dollman Testimonial Year.
All proceeds from the sale of this book will support the Phil Dollman Testimonial Year, Exeter Foundation and Devon Air Ambulance.

Printed by Ingram's Lightning Source

Photography: Phil Mingo, Pinnacle Photo Agency. www.ppauk.com
Recipes: Checked and edited by Debbie Vanstone, Mad Cakes Exeter. www.madcakesexeter.co.uk
Design: Ali Myer, Myer Consultancy. www.alimyer.com

Lightning Source UK Ltd.
Milton Keynes UK
UKHW050647071218
333564UK00005B/18/P

9 781527 230866